What Others Are Saying...

"An excellent book that's interesting and fun to read and presents key principles that apply to business, family, church and all facets of life. I was unable to stop until I finished."
　　　　　　　-David Channel, Human Resources Manager
　　　　　　　　　　Wright Medical Technology, Inc.

"A real home run! Designed for the people who matter most...our front line."
　　　　　　　　　　-Rick Root, Director
　　　　　　　　　　White Water

"...makes it easy to absorb great wisdom about getting and keeping those very important people, our customers."
　　　　　　　　　　-Springfield Business Journal

"An excellent book that is fun and interesting for our top executives to our hourly associates!"
　　　　　　　　　　-Paul Wakim, Manager
　　　　　　　　　　Training & Development
　　　　　　　　　　Western Auto

"It's excellent! Your use of a story format makes it extremely interesting."
　　　　　　　　　　-Curt Underwood, Vice President
　　　　　　　　　　of Training and Sales
　　　　　　　　　　Magna Bank

"Today's employees are enlightened with new concepts and empowered when they learn to apply the concepts on their jobs. WOOING empowers and energizes employees as they secure their futures with customer focus. I will recommend WOOING to my clients!"
　　　　　　　　　　-Brian Molitor, C.E.O
　　　　　　　　　　Molitor, Inc.

WOOING CUSTOMERS BACK

WOOING CUSTOMERS BACK is available in quantity discounts for bulk purchases. For more information on WOOING and accompanying training resources developed especially for WOOING readers, please see the order form in back or contact us at:

Advance Mark Publishing
PO Box 3175
Springfield, MO 65808
417/883-7434

WOOING CUSTOMERS BACK

MARK HOLMES

Advance Mark Publishing
Springfield, Missouri

WOOING CUSTOMERS BACK
How To Give Great Service And Increase Your Own Success

Published by Advance Mark Publishing

Copyright © 1994, 1995 J. Mark Holmes

First Printing: October, 1994
Second Printing: January, 1995
Third Printing: May, 1995, revised
Manufactured in the United States of America

Library of Congress Cataloging in Publication Data

Holmes, Mark.
     Wooing customers back : how to give great service and increase your own success / Mark Holmes. -- Rev. ed. -- Springfield, Mo.: Advance Mark Pub., 1995.
     p. cm.
     Preassigned LCCN: 94-79428.
     ISBN 0-9643828-1-4

     1. Customer service. 2. Management. I. Title.

HF5415.5.H65 1995   658.8'12
                                                        QBI95-20207

Contents

Introduction
Who Should Read This Book?

This story is written for anyone at any level serving the customer. Especially anyone wanting the enormous personal advantages resulting from increasing service where they work.

The real effectiveness for any organization tomorrow, will be how well they develop loyal customers today. Consequently, the quickest route for you to gain promotions, rewards and new opportunities will be to learn vital customer satisfaction skills and attitudes. Successful businesses will aggressively develop and seek out people that are service sharp.

What you read in *WOOING CUSTOMERS BACK* is a compilation of service wisdom I learned working with some of the best organizations anywhere. Further, you are presented with insights I have gained from monitoring thousands of customer survey responses, helping you avoid some of the most damaging mistakes.

WOOING CUSTOMERS BACK is written as a fable so that the most effective ideas can be explained in a concise and enjoyable style, and yet stimulate the thinking of anyone reading it. Summaries of major points are conveniently located throughout the book.

My aim is that these ideas will greatly benefit you and your organization.

My advice is that you consistently work at these principles to master them.

My hope is that you will enjoy the experience and accomplish your own goals.

Wanting To Succeed

A certain young man, John Wright, wanted to succeed in business very badly. So he read anything he could find.

All the sources gave the same advice--give great customer service.

John wondered whether giving great service benefited him personally or just the company he worked for. While he wasn't a manager yet, he wanted to be--and wondered what to teach people about great service.

So John searched for the best customer service he could locate. He ran down every lead he read or heard about.

The search produced disappointing results after six months. No one could put great service simply. They complicated great service with models, theories and too much research.

And none of the companies were willing to explain whether giving great service benefited employees or just the company.

John wondered if the principles of great service *could* be simplified. He also wondered whether anyone would share them. "Maybe customer service was just another popular business fad," he thought.

Then twelve years ago, while on vacation, John read about a very successful businessman. A man who attributed his company's success to wooing customers back with the best service.

John Wright wanted to meet this man. He wanted to learn his secrets. This is his story.

Finding The Best Customer Service

The curtains were drawn tight and not a sliver of sunshine peeked in. The red six and two zeros glared at me from the alarm clock. I love the early morning, but my wife Bev would rather stay tucked in bed.

As she slept I snuck away to the beach--it's stunning at sunrise. I sauntered along the shoreline for over an hour before plunking down in front of our hotel. Waves slapped against the shoreline and trickled back. Some traveled far enough to puddle underneath my seat and disappear into the magnificent sands of St. Thomas.

"Paper, morning paper," a cheery young man announced walking up to me.

This young man had a curious pleasantness about him that I liked instantly. He was mysterious. Not in some skittish way, but his beaming smile and enthusiasm were contagious.

"Care to read the paper this morning, sir? It's loaded with recent news from around the world," he smiled and said.

"Sure," I said smiling back.

As I fumbled around for change amidst my room key and small bottle of suntan oil he asked, "Enjoying your stay, sir?"

"Oh yes, very much, it's gorgeous here. Do you ever tire of it?"

"Never. You can't take this beauty for granted."

"You seem to enjoy your job. I'll admit, I didn't expect to find someone as happy as you working this morning on the beach."

He chuckled and replied, "Better to be happy than gloomy they say--it sure feels better anyway. Well, I better get going, nice chatting with you. My name's Johnny and I'll be here each morning about this time if you want a paper."

"That's easy to remember, my name's John," I chuckled.

Johnny smiled saying, "John, thank you and I hope to see you again."

I watched him walk on for a moment while still struck by his high spirited attitude. Turning to the paper a headline caught my eye: <u>FROM PAPER BOY TO ISLAND'S WEALTHIEST</u>. I read the story.

"Go to any Frank Christi company and you'll see customers coming in steady streams--literally. They're setting volume records again, seven years running.

Why do customers keep coming back? And why do they tell so many friends about their Christi experience?

Because they get good prices? No. They pay a little more according to the customers we talked to. Are Christi businesses more convenient? No. In fact they travel a little out of the way.

Then why do customers come? What has been the prescription for such enormous success?

According to Frank Christi, 'Customers keep coming because we woo them back with great service. We have three secrets to our service and we call them:

Three Woos For Great Service. The three Woos have a tremendous impact on our business because they put the focus on the customer. Plus, the Woos place emphasis on individual success as the company succeeds. So there's something in it for everyone,' Mr. Christi explained. "

I wondered if this could be true and how the three Woos could work for me? But, would Mr. Christi be willing to share his secrets? I was hopeful.

Grasping the paper I jogged back to the room. I noisily bustled in and the clamor woke Bev.

"What's wrong?" she asked.

"I read an article about a very successful businessman and I'm calling to see if he'll meet with me," I said reaching for the phone book.

Sitting up now, Bev said, "On our vacation?"

"Yes," I added, "Bev, you know I've been searching for the secrets to great customer service. I may have found them in a Mr. Christi. I'm hoping he'll meet."

My call to Christi Enterprises was answered in

two rings. "Good morning, Christi Enterprises this is Muriel, how may I help you?" she said cheerfully. I could picture a smile on her face.

"My name is John Wright and I just read an interesting article on your founder, Mr. Christi. I realize this is probably a bother, but, I would like to visit with Mr. Christi about the article. Is that possible?"

"Mr. Wright, you're not a bother whatsoever. In fact, Mr. Christi just walked in, let me put you through."

"Hello, this is Frank," he answered with a pleasant tone of voice.

After telling him what I was calling about he agreed to meet.

"Tomorrow then," Mr. Christi confirmed, "10 a.m. at my office. Stay on the line and Muriel will give you directions. I look forward to meeting you."

Understanding What Matters
About Success

To no surprise, Muriel was just as friendly and caring in person as by phone. She was sharply dressed which complimented her warm smile. She showed me in and Mr. Christi was standing ready to greet me.

"Very nice to meet you, Mr. Wright. Please have a seat," Mr. Christi offered as he shook my hand.

His smile and warmth put me instantly at ease. He looked the part of an islander. His natural dark tan was highlighted by a canary yellow sport shirt and khaki pants. The lines on his face suggested he was in his early sixties. In good shape for his age too.

"It's my pleasure to meet you Mr. Christi," I said.

"Please, call me Frank," suggested Mr. Christi.

"And please call me John," I replied.

Mr. Christi laughed and said, "Now that we

have the formalities taken care of I'd like to know why you wanted to see me."

"Well, I was fascinated by the article and I'd like to know how you became so successful."

"We better get one thing clear up front John, don't be impressed with me or what I've acquired."

Then he leaned across his desk and said very seriously, "The measure of a person's success is not found in what they've accomplished, or, in wealth gained. Rather, look at who they are and what they stand for. What really matters to me John, is that the people I work with count it a privilege to have known me. That they became better, happier, more prosperous because of my influence in their life."

I could tell that he was a very wise man. His words were piercing and sincere. For a moment I absorbed his explanation. "So, you've tried to be a role model instead of a success story, is that right?" I asked.

"Precisely, John," he exclaimed. "I believe that it's important to have a successful career--but it's more important to make a difference in someone's life. A wise man once said, *A good name is more desirable than great riches."*

"In the article yesterday you referred to Three Woos For Great Service. What are they exactly?"

"I'd be happy to share them with you, on one condition."

"What's that?" I wondered.

"That as you prosper from the three Woos, you will share them with anyone who can benefit."

"I will if they work."

Frank chuckled, "I like you John, you're an independent thinker. And as for the Woos, I think you'll find they work for anyone. Now then, let's go down to the conference room--I want to show you the first Woo there."

The First Woo: Pick Up The Ball When It's Dropped

The first thing I noticed walking into the conference room were three huge words written in red on the grease board. The words *Somebody, Nobody* and *Everybody* looked like they were placed there for a training session. I also noticed a football on the large mahogany conference table. "What's a football doing on the conference table?" I asked laughing.

"Oh we play catch in here when we're on break," Frank said laughing. "Really, I use it when I'm explaining our first Woo to new associates. Let me give it to you now. Write down the three words you see on the board."

I grabbed the journal I'd brought for notes and quickly jotted them down:

```
Somebody
Nobody
Everybody
```

Then Frank grabbed the football and dropped it on the floor. When it stopped rolling around he said, "Now, if we're both on the same team and *Somebody* on our team drops the ball and *Nobody* picks it up--*Everybody* loses! Right?"

I nodded.

"Here's the bottom line John," Frank said as he picked up the ball. "Whether you're the clerk or the manager, or even the owner--you lose and you lose big when no one picks up a dropped ball.

"But get this too," Frank said dropping the ball again, "when *Somebody* drops the ball and *Somebody Else* picks it up--*Everybody* wins!"

"Are you saying to pick up the ball when you weren't the one who dropped it?"

"Yes," Frank stressed fervently.

★ ★ ★

When Somebody Drops The Ball And Somebody Else Picks It Up-- Everybody Wins!

★ ★ ★

"Why?" I wanted to know.

"Because, helping and cooperating together is the key to reaching your individual and team goals better and faster.

"You see, when teammates push against each other, or they don't pick up dropped balls--they harm themselves and the team because they're negatively affecting the customer's experience with the company.

"Do you see the result?" Frank asked without expecting an answer. "The result is, the customer's satisfaction is lessened and the company doesn't perform as well."

"I agree with what you've said Frank, but I'm having trouble with what picking up the ball has to do with the customer's satisfaction. Maybe if you had an example I could relate better."

"As a matter of fact I do. And it's a true story.

"I tried a restaurant not too far from here for the first time several years ago. It was around two-thirty in the afternoon and understandably slow in the restaurant. There were only two customers and about eight waiters and waitresses.

"A waitress came over and asked for my order. But she wasn't very friendly and it seemed she didn't really want to be there. I placed my order and asked for a glass of ice tea and water. Then, she walked to the drink station and immediately began talking to her co-workers. I thought she'd return promptly with my tea and water, instead she continued visiting. Several minutes went by . . . it felt like fifteen. She just kept talking and--"

"You mean you didn't leave with service like *that*?" I questioned with surprise.

"Well, let me tell you the rest of the story. I waited another three to four minutes to see if she'd quit talking and take care of me. She didn't, so I did start to leave. But, I noticed someone in the restaurant staring at me and I couldn't figure out why. You know who it was?"

"No, who?", I asked anxiously.

"The young lady bussing tables. As she diligently cleaned and straightened she'd stop about every thirty seconds, rest her hands on her hips and look with real concern at my table. Then, she'd look

25

in the direction of the drink station and then back at my table again. She did that three times. Suddenly, she picked up the gray dish tub, walked over and set it down by my table. Then she smiled and asked, *Sir, did you order anything to drink?* I told her, *Yes, I ordered water and ice tea but my waitress hasn't brought it over.*

"She glanced momentarily at the drink station again and offered, *Would you like me to get it for you?* I answered, *Yes, I would appreciate that thank you.*

"She went to the drink station and poured my tea and water. Unfortunately, the waitress never noticed her. She was too preoccupied visiting. When the young busser returned, she placed my tea and water on the table. Then she said these incredible words, *Sir, I'm sorry it took us so long to get this to you. I hope you have a nice day and thank you for coming.*"

"She could have blamed it on the waitress," I blurted without thinking.

"Yes she could have John. But, that wouldn't solve my problem--and it would have sounded unprofessional. I can tell you this, if she hadn't picked up the ball I would have left. Then they would have lost my business--possibly forever. Most customers never give you a second chance.

"Can you see the tremendous advantages of cooperating with your teammates?" Frank asked.

"I do now. I can see how *not* picking up the ball loses customers--and when you lose customers you lose much needed business. And what gets me is how losing customers affects my personal wages or maybe my job security."

"That's right. The more successful your company is the more opportunities and rewards they can offer you."

"Frank, I'm really struck by the busser's attitude toward you."

"I was too, so much so that I left her a healthy tip and sent a letter of praise to her boss. But that's not all. Because that young lady Picked Up The Ball her restaurant gained too."

"How?" I questioned.

"Well, they got my lunch revenue when they

almost got nothing. Plus, get this, several weeks later I selected them to cater two employee banquets--"

"Wow."

"Wait there's more," Frank said with excitement. "I took countless business guests there and recommended the restaurant to friends for years. The loads of business they received from me, my company, and my friends helped pay the employee's wages, pay raises, helped create new jobs--and increased job security."

"But, what if the ball's dropped and it's not your job?"

"That's a good question. In many companies the line is drawn in the sand pretty clearly and it may not be permissible to step out of your boundaries. Or, you may not be trained to do a teammate's job. So in either of those cases I wouldn't recommend Picking Up The Ball until you know it's okay."

"Do you still go to that seafood restaurant?"

"Yes I still go there, but, now I have a vested interest because I own it," Frank chuckled.

"Really?"

"Yes, you'll have to go, it's a magnificent seafood place. Ask for Louise, she was promoted to General Manager one year ago yesterday. She used to be the busser I just told you about!"

"You're kidding," I said startled.

"No, one in the same."

"Boy, she did well for herself."

"That's right she did. Louise is a real team player and has a great caring attitude toward her customers. Exactly the qualities most business people, including myself, look for in the people they promote."

Ring. . . .ring. Frank answered his phone, "Hello. That's okay Tom, go ahead."

Then Frank covered the phone and said, "Pardon me just a minute John, but I was expecting this call and it won't take long."

I started to leave for a few minutes but Frank motioned for me to stay.

While Frank handled his call I realized that the ideas I was getting from him would help me and my company succeed. So I made a list of what he'd said about Picking Up The Ball.

Summary/Picking Up The Ball

1. You lose when no one Picks Up The Ball. Because, the customer leaves and may not come back. This affects your future wages, job opportunities and security.

2. Blaming your teammate solves nothing for the customer. And blame sounds unprofessional.

3. Picking Up The Ball woos the customer back and increases your company's success. The more successful your company is, the more opportunities they can offer you in promotions and rewards.

4. Picking Up The Ball can result in customers telling their friends about your company. This increases business which then creates more opportunities for employees.

Summary (cont'd)

5.   You should be adequately trained and know that it's okay with your manager before you cross job lines and Pick Up The Ball.

6.   Being a team player and having a caring attitude toward the customer are qualities that help get you promoted.

Knock The Walls Down

While Frank was on the phone I overheard him say, *You know what to do Thomas, lead them to knock the walls down. Let me know how it turns out soon.*

"John, again I apologize for the interruption but I had to speak with one of my managers."

"That's alright Frank. If you don't mind me asking, what did you mean by, knock the walls down?"

"No, I don't mind you asking--in fact it relates well to our discussion about teamwork and customer satisfaction. What we mean by walls are situations that separate people. Walls are common and *inevitable* unfortunately. Literally, I've witnessed walls built at all levels between people, like:

- Between associates
- Associates to managers
- Managers to managers
- Between departments and
- From one store to another."

"How do walls affect a company or a team?" I asked, wanting to know more.

"That's a good question," Frank complimented. "Let's take Thomas' case because it's having a predictable impact. Two of his departments aren't communicating like they should and it's affecting everyone's work quality. And their teamwork is lousy. They bicker, they're uncooperative and spread gossip about each other like crazy. Of course, the biggest impact is the one it's having on the customer," Frank said shaking his head in disappointment.

"How does the customer know they've built walls between themselves?"

"Well, let me ask you a question. Have you ever felt tension when you entered a business?"

After thinking I answered, "Yes, as a matter of fact I felt and saw tension between two tellers at my bank just before we left."

"What happened?" Frank wondered.

"They were upset with another teller who'd apparently taken too long for break. Both of them complained openly during my transaction. This made me uncomfortable and quite honestly, a little hacked off because of their inattentiveness to me."

"Great example. *Customers can feel tension between employees,* or in your case see it. And we know that tension between teammates reduces the level of service to the customer. Just think how many dropped balls aren't getting picked up between those two departments of ours. That means our sales are suffering too."

"What are walls caused by?" I wondered.

Frank named four common wall builders and I jotted them down.

★ ★ ★

Customers Can Feel Tension Between Employees

★ ★ ★

Sources of wall builders include:

1. Enemy number one is blame. Blame never solves problems, it makes them worse. Because it takes our attention off possible solutions and steers it to pointing fingers.
2. Disagreements or conflicts that go unresolved and spread.
3. Looking at ourselves as several different teams versus one team. This causes inner rivalries and conflicting goals.
4. Petty jealousies over break times, perceptions of easier jobs, one department getting something another department doesn't...can build walls.

"Are you sure you haven't visited where I work?" I laughed. "I've seen all four happen--and there are some mighty big walls built up between our people. What do you have to do to knock down walls?"

With experience in his voice Frank replied,

"There are three keys to knocking down walls:

1st Key:

Value each teammate because you need their help to reach your individual and team goals. With their assistance you'll reach your goals more quickly and more effectively.

2nd Key:

Settle disputes, differences and misunderstandings quickly. The cost of constructing walls between us is too great, on ourselves and our customers. Walls increase tensions, damage service to customers, lessen job satisfaction and reduce our work quality.

KEYS (cont'd)

3rd Key:

> Do your part to cooperate and help. Realize you are important. Your role is vital to the company's success. Others are depending on you so you have an awesome responsibility to fulfill."

When he finished I commented, "Frank these are all so practical, anyone can do them!"

"That's right and--."

"But you know," I injected, "this third key surprises me a little."

"Why's that?" Frank questioned curiously.

"Well, do you really believe each person is *vital* to the team's success?"

"Absolutely. Let me use a story that illustrates the tremendous value of each person. It goes like this. Once there was a certain beautiful bird that perched high atop a tree. One day a man walked by carrying a box. The beautiful bird asked, *What are you carrying in the box?* *Oh,* the man replied, *I have nice plump worms in here. In fact, I'll trade you one of my nice, plump worms for one of your beautiful feathers.*

"The beautiful bird thought about the man's offer and agreed. *What can it hurt to give up just one of my feathers,* he said. As the bird ate the worm he thought about how hard he searched for his food each day. *It's much easier and quicker to trade a feather for a plump worm,* he thought aloud. So each day for the next several weeks the bird traded the man one feather for one worm. And then one day, the beautiful bird looked down and discovered that he no longer had enough feathers to fly.

"That's how I feel about each of our associates," Frank said. "It takes each of them to help us fly."

"I've never thought about my importance to the team," I acknowledged. "But now I see that I am important to my company. If I don't give my all it's going to affect everyone on my team--they're counting on me. Is that what you're saying?"

"Yes, yes that's it exactly," Frank answered with a smile.

"Our talk this morning has been very beneficial and it's taught me a lot. Now I'd like to know what the Second Woo For Great Service is. Can you tell me?"

Frank laughed saying, "I'd love to discuss it with you. But I have another appointment in a few minutes. If you'd like, come back same time tomorrow and we'll talk about the second Woo."

"Fantastic, I'd love to."

I thanked Frank and excused myself.

On the trip back to the hotel I considered what I'd learned from Frank. It was so practical and wise. "He's right, one of the best ways to help yourself is to knock down the walls so that you can help your company, your teammates and customers," I thought outloud.

I quickly summarized my notes.

Summary/Knocking The Walls Down

1. Remember customers can feel tension. And tensions reduce your service which can cause the customer to go elsewhere.

2. You should Knock Down Walls because they can decrease your job satisfaction, and cripple teamwork.

3. The four sources of walls are: blame, disagreements, viewing ourselves as several different teams and petty jealousies.

4. You can Knock The Walls Down by valuing your teammates, settling your disputes quickly and by doing your part to cooperate and help because others are depending on you.

5. Your value to your team and the company is enormous. You have an awesome responsibility to your teammates--they're counting on you.

The Second Woo:
Go Way Beyond Customer Expectations

"Good morning, John," Muriel said as pleasantly as yesterday. "Go right in, Frank is expecting you."

"Island greetings to you John. How are you today?" Frank asked.

"Thank you, I'm doing great for three hours of sleep. I thought about our conversation much of the night," I admitted.

"You've got to be kidding. Do you feel like doing this today?"

"I wouldn't miss it. Can you tell me what the second Woo is now?"

"Sure--."

"By the way," I interrupted smiling, "why do you call your three beliefs Woos?"

Frank chuckled, "No reason really. We like to create fun at work and one of our associates suggested the Three Woos--because I was always talking about wooing the customer back. It was a great idea and it stuck.

"Now we give annual Woo Awards, have Woo coaching sessions for struggling associates, and we give Wooies to employees receiving a customer compliment! Things some companies see as silly we do to break up the routine.

"Now John, I've decided to let you see the second Woo at work for yourself, at our restaurant the Crab Shell. Muriel has already called a cab."

"Isn't that where, uh, Louise now works as the General Manager?"

"Yes, the one and only Louise--the former busser."

"But, how will I know what to look for? What if I miss it?" I asked with concern.

"The second Woo is, Go Way Beyond Customer Expectations. Now go *see it through the customer's eyes* and enjoy yourself please," Frank urged.

The thirty minute drive to the Crab Shell was postcard photography at its best. The magnificent Caribbean and the glimmering sandy beaches of

St. Thomas were hypnotizing. The cab stopped and I walked to the greeter stand just inside the front door.

"Welcome sir," said a friendly young lady, "it's a pleasure to have you at the Crab Shell today. Will there be one for lunch?"

She made me feel welcome. "Yes, just one please," I replied. I peeked around the corner and noticed that the tables were filling quickly.

I waited just a minute when another young lady walked up and suggested cheerily, "May I show you to your table now?"

"Yes, thank you. You sure are bubbly today-- did you get a pay raise?" I asked chuckling.

The young lady laughed, "No sir. But, I wouldn't turn one down either." She showed me my table and said smiling, "Thank you for coming today-- have a great meal."

In a minute the waiter came over and greeted me pleasantly--something I'd grown accustomed to here. After I ordered I sat and just watched Frank's people-- *through the customer's eyes* like he urged.

Waiters and waitresses smiled and spoke to

customers. Even at tables they weren't assigned they cheerily acknowledged the customer. Obviously, they felt every customer was *their* customer. Amazingly even the bussers--who usually don't interact with customers at all in most restaurants--smiled and spoke briefly.

Frank's associates were very good at customer service. And the meal was great too.

After finishing, I made quite a list about what I'd seen.

At Frank's restaurant I noticed that:
1. Associates went out of their way to be personable and friendly.
2. Associates were energetic and visibly cheerful, often smiling.
3. Associates seemed to genuinely care about your experience at the Crab Shell. Their caring attitude made me feel important.

LIST (cont'd)

4. Associates considered every customer theirs--doing whatever they needed to make the customer's experience worth repeating.
5. Going Way Beyond Customer Expectations was working...

"Sir, how was your meal and the service today?" a distinctly dressed woman suddenly appeared and asked.

I looked up at her name tag, "Louise," I blurted, astonished to see her at my table.

"Yes, can I help you?" Louise asked politely.

Louise looked to be in her late thirties. Long flowing jet black hair accentuated her otherwise ordinary looks. Her personal warmth created an instant likability and comfortableness.

"Louise, I'm John Wright and Mr. Christi told me quite a bit about you."

"All good I hope," she replied chuckling. "Frank told me you'd be coming, he just didn't mention when. He said you're learning the Three Woos For Great Service."

"Right, and I came here to learn about the second Woo, Go Way Beyond Customer Expectations. Can you explain it to me?"

"Sure, I'd be glad to," Louise answered smiling. "Let's go to my office and visit."

Louise got up, took my check and said, "Your meal is on me today John."

Her office was upstairs down a narrow hallway. Louise offered a seat and then wanted to know, "So what did you think about Picking Up The Ball When It's Dropped?"

"I think Frank's right, you better be willing to Pick Up The Ball if you want customers to return. And Frank got me to see clearly, that the opportunities I'll have as an employee are directly linked to the successfulness of my company."

Louise nodded, "Frank's quite a teacher and everything he shares is so useful and sensible. I'll tell

47

you what makes Frank's message so powerful to me. It's his belief in the importance of each associate, and his belief in each associate's vital role in the customer's satisfaction," Louise said with conviction.

"Do you really believe that a front-line employee has that much to do with the customer coming back?" I inquired.

"You're crazy or shortsighted if you don't believe it," Louise shot back. "And basically that's a problem in most businesses--they undervalue the importance of their front-line associates."

"I'll tell you this much," Louise continued emphasizing, "a clerk, a bank teller or a waitress has more opportunity to woo the customer back than their manager ever will."

"So that's why you want every Christi associate to know how to Go Way Beyond Customer Expectations," I noted.

"Exactly," Louise answered, smiling.

"Louise, when I walked the beach this morning I was wondering what really causes customers to leave and not come back?"

★ ★ ★

A Clerk, Bank Teller Or Waitress Has More Opportunity To Woo The Customer Back Than Their Manager Ever Will

★ ★ ★

Louise sat up slightly in her chair and said, "You want to know something, now this is interesting. Get this. The number one reason customers don't come back is because they felt they got treated indifferently."

"Really?"

"Yes, about sixty-eight percent of the time, *indifference,* which basically means an uncaring attitude, is the reason customers go elsewhere.

"Now obviously, product, price and convenience are still important--but they're not the main reason the customer gives you their loyalty. The main reason is *you* and how well *you* demonstrate that you care about their business."

"Wow! *I'm* the critical link in the customer coming back. What you're saying is that our product and price can be real attractive to customers, but my *attitude* is what either brings them back or drives them away."

"Precisely," Louise insisted.

"Is that what it means, then, to Go Way Beyond Customer Expectations--to care?"

"Yes, in part. We believe John, that to give great service you must *intentionally* show a caring attitude."

"Intentionally?" I questioned, wondering what she meant.

"Absolutely. Let me explain an intentionally caring attitude this way. Think about visiting a church for the first time. For most churches, the problem is not that the people in the church don't care about you being there. The problem is getting their members to show it outwardly. Many businesses are like that too. Their associates care, but they don't show it outwardly to the customer like they should," Louise clarified.

"Around here we like to say, Customers Are Watching So Give Them A Great Show!"

"That's good," I said smiling while jotting it down. "So if your job deals with the customer you're basically always on stage aren't you?"

"Yes, you could say that," Louise answered with a gleam in her eye obviously pleased with my point. "And since the customer is watching our every action,

★ ★ ★

Customers Are Watching
So Give Them
A Great Show!

★ ★ ★

we've got to show them an intentionally caring attitude."

"How?" I asked outloud.

"Well, there are four important ways to show a caring attitude. In fact, I'd write them down if I were you because you'll want to review them again later.

"The four ways to show a caring attitude are:

1. Treat your customer spectacularly.

   Result: they'll come back to you first.

2. Do your job right the first time and set high standards for yourself.

   Result: taking a little extra time to double-check your work eliminates inconvenience to the customer later.

3. Complete your job when promised. Follow up when you said you would.

   Result: this makes your customer feel like they can depend on you.

LIST (cont'd)

4. Perform dozens of little out-of-the-way acts to please.

   Result: customers will reward your Going Beyond Expectations with repeat business. "

"You do have an example of how caring works, don't you?" I hoped.

"Yes, as a matter of fact let me tell you the story of a young man that started mowing yards for extra money. On the young man's first job his dad arranged to help him load up when he was done.

"As the young man mowed the last patch of grass his dad arrived. After he and his dad loaded the mowers, the young man hopped in the car and said, *Let's go.* His dad replied, *Not so fast, let's look at your work first* Upon surveying his son's work he asked, *Are you sure you're done?* That startled the young man and he replied *Yes, why?* His dad instructed, *Well, come here for a minute.* "

"I like this story already." I said.

"I thought you would. Let me go on," Louise requested kindly.

"Now the young man's dad pointed out where trees, corners of the house and several curbs weren't trimmed very well. The young man explained, *But they didn't ask me to trim.* That didn't matter to the young man's dad. He said, *Do your job right the first time and do more than your customer expects and you'll always get asked back.*"

"Then, to the young man's horror, his dad told him to mow and trim the whole yard again--as if grass were still there. So very reluctantly, he did.

"His dad showed him how to do the little extras that make a lawn look really sharp. Plus he taught him the habit of quickly double-checking his work. When they were done, his father encouraged him to talk to the customer. So the young man asked his customer, *How does your yard look sir?* The customer replied, *It looks great, nice job young man.* The young man then asked, *Is there anything special I can do for you?* The customer said smiling, *No, not today thank you.* The customer was very pleased and recommended the young man to several friends. Soon the young man built a very successful lawn mowing business--because he got good at Going Way Beyond Customer Expectations," Louise related.

"And don't forget his dad's influence," I suggested. "When the value the young man placed on his customer's satisfaction increased, so did his successfulness."

"That's right," Louise said.

Then Louise laughed heartily like she'd just remembered a funny joke. She sat back in her chair and said, "I've got to tell you," she said still laughing, "what Frank did at one of our businesses."

"What?" I asked curiously.

"Well, this particular business had been receiving some pretty disturbing customer complaints like: *Your people don't seem to care about my business; Employees were too pre-occupied to notice me; Your clerk was unmotivated and impersonal, etc.*"

"What did Frank do?" I was dying to know.

"Well first, he went into the business and

replaced all the light bulbs in the breakroom with six candles. Then, he gathered all the associates into the breakroom, lit the candles and said, *You'll notice that I took out the light bulbs and I'm replacing them with these six candles. I'd like the candles to represent our customers and their importance to each of our continued livelihoods. Now for the next six days, I'd like you as you sit here at lunch, to think about that.*

"Then each day for the next six days, Frank went in at lunch, blew out one candle and took it with him. On the sixth day, with the breakroom in total darkness, our associates got the message about the value of each customer!"

"I bet they turned their service around?" I commented chuckling at Frank's wit.

"You bet they did," Louise answered. "After Frank's lesson we gave them some Woo coaching sessions and retaught everyone how to *look and sound like you're ready to serve.*"

"Look and sound like they're ready to serve?" I echoed wanting to learn more as I wrote it down.

★ ★ ★

Look And Sound Like You're Ready To Serve

★ ★ ★

"Certainly," Louise insisted. "We want our associates doing things that show the customer they're ready and anxious to help. If you don't show an interest in your customer then your customer won't show an interest in you."

"You're right," I touted. "I've been in too many businesses where the associates come across as if it's a chore to wait on you. Like you're putting them out.

"But how does a person look and sound like they're ready to serve?" I wondered.

"Follow five tips. Here, let me show you," Louise said reaching for the placard they were printed on.

Louise held them up while I made notes.

How to look and sound like you're ready to serve:
1. Smile on the phone and in person
2. Make friendly eye contact (in person)
3. Have a friendly, warm tone of voice
4. Make personable conversation without detaining them
5. Give your undivided attention to each customer--put aside other tasks

"Why smiling?"

"Because *a smile is the closest distance between you and your customer.* Smiling makes you seem more approachable and friendly to the customer.

"Obviously," Louise continued, "customers prefer to be waited on by cheerful, peppy people--and you can't convey either if you're scowling or look gloomy."

"You make a very interesting and valid case for smiling. Would you mind going over the other four briefly too?" I wanted to learn more.

"Be glad to. Second, make eye contact with your customer--not with your order ticket or the cash register. Third, have a friendly, warm tone of voice. Fourth, make personable conversation without detaining them. In other words, strike up brief, pleasant conversation if you can. Fifth, give your undivided attention to the customer."

"You're undivided attention? For instance?" I wondered outloud.

"For instance, when you're preoccupied stocking, counting inventory, doing paperwork, visiting with a teammate--you should drop what you're doing as promptly as possible and turn your attention to the customer. If you've ever experienced someone who wasn't eager to end a personal conversation, or, put aside stocking to wait on you--you know how unimportant it makes you feel."

"You're certainly right, it's happened to me several times--and I felt like I got the cold shoulder."

"That's because you did," Louise confirmed. "You see, when we stay preoccupied with busy work while trying to wait on the customer at the same time, it signals the customer that they're not very important to you."

That made me remember something. "You're not going to believe what happened a few years ago when I shopped around for a car loan. It's unbelieveable, at one bank the new accounts representative I spoke to never stopped typing while she answered my questions. It was rude and I felt like she really didn't want my business."

"What did you do?" Louise asked with a tone of voice reserved for times when you know the answer already.

"I left of course."

Louise shook her head and sighed.

"There's one possible exception to looking and sounding like you're ready to serve," I noted. "You can't do it when you're super busy, can you?"

"You can't?" Louise repeated seriously. "Well let me ask you something. Does it take any longer to be friendly and caring than it does to be impersonal or rude?"

"No."

"Of course not. So if you only have twenty seconds with each customer, use each second to create a positive experience they'll want to repeat. Look, your customer doesn't care how busy you are with other customers, or for that matter how busy you are with all your job duties. What your customer cares about is *how well you're going to treat them--busy or not.*"

"That's a fantastic point, Louise. When you're swamped you should still give friendly, caring service."

Louise nodded affirmingly and smiled.

"Louise, you and Frank have convinced me that looking out for the customer is the best way to look out for myself. Going Way Beyond Customer Expectations woos customers back and makes my company and myself more successful. And it's good to see that it's easy enough to do right now. I don't have to wait.

"I think I'm ready for the third Woo now. Will you tell me what it is?"

"I could," Louise chuckled, "but for you to

understand it completely you need Frank to explain. I'm sure he's got something special reserved for the third Woo. Its made hundreds of associates at least twice as successful as they would have been--me included."

I thanked Louise for her help and excused myself. The points she'd made about Going Way Beyond Customer Expectations were very good.

Summary/Going Way Beyond
Customer Expectations

1. Remember that every customer is *your* customer. Go out of your way to be personable and friendly. Your role is critical in Wooing The Customer Back.

2. Intentionally show a caring attitude. Not caring is the number one reason the customer leaves and goes to your competition.

3. To show you care you should: treat customers spectacularly, do your job right the first time, complete your job as promised and go out of your way to please.

4. To look and sound like you're ready to serve follow five tips: smile, make friendly eye contact, speak in a kind tone of voice, make personable conversation and give your undivided attention.

Summary (cont'd)

5. When you're super busy still give each customer your very best. Because, it doesn't take any longer to be friendly and caring than it does to be rude or indifferent.

6. Anyone can easily Go Way Beyond Customer Expectations. You will be more successful and have greater opportunities if you do.

Wooing Customers Back

Before going back to the hotel though, something troubled me. I wondered whether Going Way Beyond Customer Expectations worked with *problem customers?* I called to see if Frank would meet before returning to the hotel. Muriel okayed it with him, but she mentioned that Frank wondered what was so important that we needed to meet now.

How To Treat Problem Customers

When Muriel showed me in Frank said, "Hi John. What's so important that you wanted to meet right now?"

"Well, I got to meet and visit with Louise and she really helped me with Going Way Beyond Customer Expectations. But, I'm curious whether it works with problem customers?"

"Did you ask Louise?" Frank wanted to know.

"No, I didn't think of it until I left."

"*Problem customers?*" Frank grimaced as if it were hard to say those words. "Well John I wouldn't know, we don't have any problem customers at Christi--we got rid of all ours several years ago."

"Pardon me?" I couldn't believe what I just heard. "You got rid of all your problem customers?" I repeated.

"Yes, we just don't allow them at Christi businesses anymore," Frank answered matter-of-factly.

Frank let that thought soak for a moment and then said, "Allow me to explain. You see, we use to have some customers we considered to be *problem customers*. Actually we *branded* them a *problem* because they complained, or insisted on a refund for no good reason.

"Unfortunately it took a complaint letter to get my attention. A complaint letter from a lady we *branded a problem customer*."

"What did she say?" I questioned wondering if he'd tell me.

"She wrote to tell me how we didn't seem to care about her business anymore. She said she was leaving and never coming back--plus she was going to tell everyone she knew how unfriendly we were."

"What did you learn from that?"

"We learned that the customers we'd branded *problem customers* were treated differently."

"How were you treating them?" I asked.

"Like a *problem*," Frank said seriously. "So we changed."

"How did you change?"

"First, we stopped looking at customers as the *problem* and began looking at what we needed to improve upon. Plus, we realized that we needed to appreciate customers who were willing to point out our inadequacies. Customers were giving us an opportunity to become the best and we weren't recognizing it."

"What did you do to stop the branding?"

"We re-branded everyone! Instead of branding some customers 'bad' they're now all branded 'good'. Rather than branding some 'jerks' they're all branded 'gems'. The point is, we now consider everyone a *valued customer*."

I made a quick note and asked, "So how did branding affect your business *before* you corrected it?"

"Many customers never survived the branding!"

"What do you mean?"

"They went to our competitors," Frank answered. "Let me tell you a quick story that explains it nicely.

★ ★ ★

Stop Looking At Customers As The Problem And Begin Looking At What To Improve Upon

★ ★ ★

"Once there was a man who moved his family from the big city to a cattle ranch. They bought some cattle, mended fence and settled in. After a few weeks one of his new neighbors came over. During their conversation the neighbor asked, *So what are you going to name your ranch?* The new rancher explained, *Well, we couldn't agree on that. I wanted to name our ranch the Big R, my wife wanted to name it the Lazy L. My son liked the name Four Square and my daughter wanted to name it The Double S. So we never could agree.* The neighbor chuckled and asked, *By the way where are your cattle? Driving up here I didn't see any.* The man embarrassingly replied, *None of them survived the branding.*"

I snickered a little at Frank's story--it made a beneficial point. "Branding loses customers," I remarked.

"Yes, and you may lose them forever."

"Forever?"

"Right, the studies on service say that when customer problems are handled unsatisfactorily the majority will not return."

"Frank I'd like to know, how do you treat customer problems *now?*"

"Another great question, John. I'll give you our four steps--you seem very interested in this."

"I am."

Frank's steps were very practical and wise.

How to treat customers with problems:

1. Listen carefully, without interrupting their explanation. Confirm specifically what they feel needs to be resolved.

2. Always apologize for any inconvenience the problem created. So many people treat customer problems like they're no big deal. But problems are inconveniences and they are very big deals to the customer.

LIST (cont'd)

3. Tell your customer *when* you will solve the problem. Be realistic, don't overstate your abilities. And then solve the problem as quickly as possible.

4. Keep your customer informed during every phase of getting their problem solved. For example, if you're going to be late let your customer know. Customers are more patient if they just know what's going on. Not keeping your customer informed is an unpardonable sin of service.

"But listen John, beyond these steps the most important thing is your own attitude. Remember, their problems aren't an attack on you or your company. Instead, they are opportunities to earn your customer's loyalty."

"Why?"

"Because effectively solving a customer's problem creates trust. Secondly, it demonstrates that you care and can be depended on to look out for their best interest. And when the customer feels that way about you, you'll get their repeat business."

"You know, I've never viewed customer problems as opportunities--just hassles. Every company has customer complaints and problems doesn't it?"

"Oh absolutely," Frank said leaning in. "But the real issue is how effectively a company and its associates handle customer problems.

"For example, do you still smile and act pleasant when a customer complains? Do you have the same positive attitude in this situation that you would if you were ringing up a big sale? Do you handle customer complaints better than your competition?"

Frank's questions were thought-provoking. And his tips were simple. I knew I could immediately use this knowledge at work with dissatisfied customers. I wished my managers and teammates could learn this too.

"I'm glad you explained this to me Frank. I understand a lot better now how to effectively handle customer problems.

"So what's the third Woo?" I asked.

Frank just laughed and said, "I'll let you discover it for yourself. Here's what we'll do. Tomorrow morning at 10 a.m. I'll send a cab and have you taken to Christi Mart--our department store. You'll discover the third Woo For Great Service there. For now, go enjoy some time with your wife. Don't forget, you're on vacation."

We both laughed and I dismissed myself saying, "Thank you for seeing me on such short notice Frank. I can't wait to learn about the third Woo tomorrow."

"You have good reason to be excited, the third Woo has increased the success of many, many people."

When I left Frank's office I highlighted his most important points.

Summary/Problem Customers

1. Don't brand anyone a problem customer. Instead, consider everyone a *valued customer*.

2. Remember, when customers are dissatisfied with how their problem is handled, most do not return.

3. Use four easy steps to effectively handle customer problems: listen without interruption-- learn what they want resolved specifically, apologize for the inconvenience, tell your customer when you'll solve their problem, and keep your customer informed of your progress.

4. Your personal attitude toward customer problems is most important. Solving customer problems are opportunities to woo them back.

5. Solving customer problems effectively, builds trust and shows you care. Customers learn they can depend on you and then give you their repeat business.

The Third Woo: Work With Tremendous Enthusiasm

Once at Christi Mart I noticed the shoe department first so I headed there.

I watched a young man waiting on several customers simultaneously. He was super busy but still pleasant and personable with everyone--amazing really.

He zipped from one customer to another smiling as he spoke. And his customers smiled back.

He noticed me and said pleasantly, "Hello sir, I'll be with you in just a moment."

It surprised me he'd be so observant under the busy circumstances.

After a few minutes he came over. "Sir, I apologize for the wait. Tell me, what kind of shoes are we looking for today?" he asked warmly.

"Well, I'm not looking for shoes exactly. My name is John Wright and Frank Christi sent me over to learn the third Woo For Great Service," I explained shaking hands.

"John, I'm James Andrews--it's good to meet you.

"Frank's quite a man," James continued. "I admire him a lot and he's really helped me become more successful."

"How did he help you?" I wanted to know.

"By teaching me the three Woos For Great Service."

"I know the first two, what's the third one?"

James glanced at his watch, "Look I'm going on break in four minutes. I'd be glad to discuss the third Woo over a soda at our cafe upstairs if you want?"

"Sounds great," I responded excitedly.

James dressed sharp. His sporty suit was complimented by spit-shined shoes and a classy tie. And James was likable, confident and enthusiastic. Qualities that reminded me of Louise.

In a few minutes James came up and took a seat at my booth.

"James how long have you worked for Frank?"

"Seven years."

"Really. In different departments I assume?"

"No, just Shoes," James answered.

"Wow. Isn't it boring doing the same job this long?" I was curious.

"Why would you think that doing the same job *has* to get boring? Actually, I'm still very enthused about my job," James said with passion.

"Enthusiasm must come easy for you," I stated.

"Are you kidding," James disagreed, "I suppose I work hardest on my enthusiasm each day."

"Why?"

"First because I need to. Second because Work With Tremendous Enthusiasm is the third Woo--and I've learned it's a key to great service and my own success."

"That's interesting, Work With Tremendous Enthusiasm is the third Woo," I repeated writing it down. "So do you think enthusiasm increases your own success at Christi?" I wanted to know.

"Without a doubt--what Frank taught me about enthusiasm made a huge impact on my achievements. All you have to do is look around at successful people and you'll find enthusiasm."

"What is enthusiasm?"

"Well Frank calls it *the winners edge,*" James said with a smile. "And it is--but if you look it up in the dictionary you'll find it means to have a zeal or fervor for something."

"But what if enthusiasm just isn't a part of your personality?" I was puzzled.

"Better not let Frank hear you say that! He'd tell you that's a bunch of bunk!"

"Why?"

"Because enthusiasm is a choice. Not something one person comes by naturally and another person doesn't. It's within your control and my control to *choose* our own attitude each day," James explained.

"And you choose enthusiasm, is that it?"

"Yes, it's that simple--anyone can do it. One of the first things Frank taught me was that people are as enthusiastic as they choose to be."

"You really take enthusiasm seriously," I observed.

★ ★ ★

People Are As Enthusiastic As They Choose To Be

★ ★ ★

"John you should too. Treating customers with enthusiasm is absolutely critical to giving great service."

"Why?"

"For three reasons," James answered without hesitation. "First is the fact that your enthusiasm tells the customer you care--and caring is essential to great service. Agreed?"

"Yes I agree, Frank and Louise made that crystal clear."

"Second, your enthusiasm gets the customer more interested in your product or service. And customers buy more when you're enthusiastic.

"Third is the fact that your enthusiasm gives the customer a better experience--one they'll want to repeat over and over. Unenthused, bored, dull attitudes give customers little reason to return."

All three points were beneficial to remember.

Why enthusiasm is important to great service:
1. Enthusiasm tells the customer you CARE
2. Customers buy more when you're enthusiastic
3. Enthusiasm gives the customer a better experience

"Those are three very interesting points," I said. "So what should you be enthusiastic about? Your product, your company, your customer. . . ."

"That's exactly right. Enthusiasm for your product, company and your customer are essential to wooing the customer back. And it's essential to seeing your own personal success multiply."

"Have you seen enthusiasm multiply your success?" I pursued.

James smiled and winked when he said, "I see it every week in my paycheck! Listen, before Frank showed me the importance of enthusiasm I muddled along here just doing average. When I *changed my outlook* my prosperity changed too--and now I control my own future."

"How's that?"

"Because now I can achieve whatever I set my mind to--you see my attitude is right. Before, my attitude controlled me, now I control my attitude."

James paused and I waited.

"When I put an emphasis on my enthusiasm," James continued, "opportunities came quicker, my sales increased and I won several company incentives. Now understand I'm not bragging, it's simply the impact enthusiasm has on anyone's successfulness."

"You sure seem to believe in the power of enthusiasm now," I commented with a smile.

"I do, because it works John."

"What were you like before you increased personal enthusiasm?"

"I was like too many other people I'm afraid. My job was just a job and I put in my time until I got to go home."

"How did Frank get your attention?"

"Well," James chuckled, "he didn't have to try

very hard. The opportunity for that happened when he received a serious customer complaint about me."

"What happened?" I wondered.

"One day I waited on a gentleman looking for basketball shoes. It had been a long day. I was tired and ready to go home--you know, basically going through the motions until I got off. After answering a few of his questions with a pretty unenthusiastic attitude he said, *You sure don't seem very excited about waiting on me today.* I snapped to attention, started smiling and said, *No sir, I'm sorry sir . . . I'm really glad you came in.*

"It was too little too late--he shrugged his shoulders and left. In a couple of days Frank got a letter from him that said, *I was treated very uncaringly by your shoe salesman, James. He didn't seem to be interested in my business at all and didn't act like he really wanted to be at work. I placed my order for twelve pairs of basketball shoes for my fifth grade team with your competitor. They got our uniform order too when you could have had it all. I don't know if I'll ever be back again.*"

Wooing Customers Back

"What did Frank do?" I asked eager to know.

"Exactly what I deserved. He reprimanded me and gave me some advice I've never forgotten."

"Advice?" I echoed.

"Yes," James replied. "Frank pointed out that getting tired or being ready to go home are normal and inevitable feelings. He said, the trick is to not let down at the customer's expense.

"Look at this for a moment, John, through *the customer's eyes*. Customer expectations don't lessen because we're at the end of our shift, or we've had a bad day. They still want to be served by caring, cheerful, enthusiastic associates."

"Great point," I admitted, "but is it very realistic to think someone can arouse enthusiasm when they're really tired and ready to go home? Maybe if you had an example of how--"

"Just so happens I do," James announced. "Do you like to play golf."

"I love it."

"Okay, let's say you come home from a rough work day, all worn out. I mean really worn out--and you're ready to hit the sofa. You don't feel like talking with your wife, mowing the yard, cleaning the car--or anything for that matter. You just want to be . . . a couch potato," James said grinning.

Chuckling I said, "I've wanted to be a couch potato several times."

"Then, let's say a friend of yours calls after you hit the sofa and invites you to play nine holes of golf before dark. What would you do?"

"I'd jump at the chance," I spouted.

"But," James said smiling, "what about wanting to hit the sofa because you're worn out from work?"

I laughed, "I see what you're saying. I have the ability to create more energy and enthusiasm for anything I want."

"Yes, that's exactly the point," James said excitedly.

"And enthusiasm," I continued, "*can* and *should* be stirred up whenever we're tired or just ready to go home. That's part of the secret to Working With Tremendous Enthusiasm, isn't it?"

James nodded.

★ ★ ★

I Have The Ability To Create More Energy And Enthusiasm For Anything I Want

★ ★ ★

"John," James began, "do you know how to tell if you're getting burned out at work and in need of an enthusiasm adjustment?"

"Not really, but I'd like to."

"Then let me tell you," James replied.

I made notes because James' list was right on target and several hit home for me. The symptoms made me consider how far I'd strayed from enthusiasm.

Symptoms of too little enthusiasm include:
1. Your job is dull, boring or tiresome
2. Dealing with customers is aggravating or bothersome
3. You are often unenergetic, unhappy or dissatisfied with your work

---

"James, have you ever known a truly enthusiastic person besides Frank?"

"Oh my yes, I've worked around lots of them."

"How did they affect your attitude?"

"Well, enthusiastic people have a positive impact

on everyone John. They put you in a cheery mood, boost your energy, give you more optimism--and enhance your life. Their enthusiasm is contagious."

"Anyone in particular at Christi Mart impact you like that?" I was curious.

"Yes, Mary did. She's the most successful salesperson ever at Christi Mart."

"Can I meet her?"

"No. She retired last year--but I can tell you her profound but simple secret to enthusiasm."

"I'd love to know, what is it?"

"Mary was *always on*," James laughed.

"What do you mean?" I wanted to know more.

"That was her personal slogan. Mary used to say, *the good Lord didn't intend for retail people to have an on/off switch--they should always be on for the customer.*

"She told me more than once, *James, don't let the customer down on your shift. They'll forget how pretty your merchandise looked, but they'll remember how well you treated them.* And it didn't matter if Mary was at the end of her shift or how tired she was, every customer got her best effort. I remember her saying, *Customers who come in at the end of your shift shouldn't get your leftovers. So be 'up' and stay 'up'*."

"Sounds like quite a lady."

"Yes," James replied with affection.

I mulled this over a few more seconds and then said, "You know James, it goes back to what you taught me earlier--anyone can choose enthusiasm if they *want* to. It's that simple isn't it?"

"Yes it is," James replied. Then he glanced at his watch and announced, "Well I've enjoyed our conversation John but I need to get back. Has this helped you any?"

"Its helped tremendously. I know now that I need renewed enthusiasm for my job. I've let my job become boring and tiresome--and it's affecting my attitude. And you've made me realize that my enthusiasm, or lack of it, will impact my successfulness wherever I work.

"It seems to me the ball's in my court now. Choose enthusiasm and get the rewards, or, live with the cost of mediocrity."

"I'm sure you'll choose the rewards," James said standing up. "John, I've enjoyed meeting and visiting with you. I better get back now--I think someone will be needing a pair of shoes," he joked.

We both laughed and he left after shaking hands and wishing me good luck.

I pondered the tremendous wisdom James shared. He was right, enthusiasm is crucial . . .

Suddenly a young lady approached my table handed me a note and said, "Excuse me Mr. Wright, but Mr. Christi left a message at the office for you and James said I'd probably still find you here."

The note said, *"John I'd like to see you when you're done if that's convenient. Please call if it's not. Thank you, Frank. "*

I was delighted that Frank wanted to meet and decided to summarize my journal before leaving.

Summary/Working With Tremendous Enthusiasm

1. Your job does not have to become dull, dreary or boring.

2. Choose to be enthusiastic each day--it's within your control to have a more cheerful outlook.

3. Enthusiasm is important to great service because: it tells the customer you CARE; customers buy more from enthusiastic salespeople, and enthusiasm gives customers a much better experience.

4. Increase your enthusiasm because it boosts your own success. Enthusiastic people get better opportunities and achieve more.

5. Getting tired or being ready to go home are normal and inevitable feelings. Overcome this with enthusiasm and caring.

6. Always be on for your customer. Be ready to serve and be ready to sell with your best.

How To Get And Keep Unlimited Enthusiasm

Frank was at Muriel's desk when I walked in. "Hello John come on in," Frank said. "I understand you got to visit with James. How did it go?"

Walking down the hall to his office I said, "Frank, James really opened my eyes to how enthusiasm makes someone more successful. But, I'm not sure about one thing."

"What's that?" Frank asked looking puzzled.

"I'm not sure I know *how* to increase my enthusiasm. After visiting with James I know I *need* to be a more enthusiastic person, I just don't know where to start. Can you help me?"

"Yes, I'd be glad to," Frank said smiling, "please have a seat. Now then, first tell me what you learned from James."

I handed my journal notes over and Frank read them.

After a few minutes he praised, "You've done a very nice job of understanding why Working With Tremendous Enthusiasm is so important to your company and yourself. So, you say you don't know where to start . . . well a story comes to mind," he said stroking his chin.

"In fact, a story that gives you three great ways to increase your enthusiasm and keep it. Listen.

"Once there was a certain village named Glum. It was named Glum because everyone who lived there was gloomy. Everyone that is except the king's son. He was an enthusiastic chap. The king's son had a positive outlook, he smiled a lot and cheerily greeted anyone who looked his way.

"Now the villagers found his enthusiasm very peculiar. They predicted he'd turn gloomy like everyone else. But, they were wrong.

"Several years later the king died and the young lad inherited the throne. Within days he issued his first decree: *I hereby commission a study to discover why everyone in Glum is so gloomy.* All the citizens were startled but complied to the king's request, of course. The researchers quickly unlocked the mystery of gloominess in Glum. The people of Glum simply fell into a rut of being dreary and cheerless.

"The young king announced his conclusions to everyone, *The bad news is, everyone in Glum is very gloomy. The good news is, no one has to stay that way. Each person can enjoy the benefits of more cheeriness and enthusiasm today, right now--if they choose to.*

"To help, he continued, *I've written three solutions to be read by everyone. I've named them, Three Keys For Increasing Your Enthusiasm Forever.*

Key Number One: Overlook Minor
Aggravations And Disappointments

Realize that aggravations and disappointments are inevitable. Bounce back quickly letting nothing negative have control over your attitude. Most irritations are minor, but, people often blow them out of proportion. A wise man once said, *No one can get under your skin if you don't let them know where to start.*

Look past the aggravations and disappointing situations in your job or home. Don't let the small stuff hinder your accomplishments and sap your enthusiasm any longer. Smart people know what to overlook and live on.

KING'S PROVERB
The Situation You're Working In Doesn't
Have To Be Working In You.

Key Number Two: Be Appreciative And Thankful

Many people stop appreciating their blessings in life. They stop noticing the beauty of a butterfly, the health of their children, the special qualities of their spouse or the advantages in their job.

Dwell today on what you should appreciate. Here, do this to help. Take a sheet of paper and list everything you can be thankful for. Think about your job, your home, your family and friends, your church-- everything. Now, look down your list. Wow! You have much to appreciate and be thankful for.

KING'S PROVERB
The Man Who Quits Being Thankful
Stops Living.

Key Number Three: Focus On
The Positives

Simply blot out what's not going right and focus on what is. Anyone can see the positives if they'll look. Look for the good in your job, your co-workers, your boss--it's there. And of course, it's there in your family too if you'll look.

My father often said, *People find what they focus on.* This is wise. If you focus on the wrongs, the mistakes, or the aggravations, that's exactly what you'll find. However, if you focus on the positives in others or in situations you face, you'll find those too. What do you most often focus on?

KING'S PROVERB
Take A Daily Inventory Of The Positives
And The Negatives Will Be Much Less Noticeable.

The young king didn't know what to expect after he circulated his Keys For Increasing Enthusiasm Forever. But once the villagers heard how practical his solutions were, they quickly replaced gloominess with enthusiasm and cheer.

A few months later the young king made another important announcement: *Upon seeing consistent cheeriness and enthusiasm in Glum, I hereby rename our village, the village of Glad.*

"Great story. Did it really happen?" I wanted to know.

"Who knows if it really happened," Frank quipped. "The important thing is to not let circumstances or other people alter your positive, cheery attitude. It's a fact, anyone *can* get and *keep* unlimited enthusiasm *if* they'll practice the three simple bits of wisdom in the story."

"From where I sit Frank, it's kind of overwhelming. I mean, I need improvement in all three of the Woos. How will I ever get it done?"

"Make the Woos a way of life and never stop improving." Frank answered wisely.

★ ★ ★

Make The Woos A Way Of Life And Never Stop Improving

★ ★ ★

"Are you saying to improve a little each day?"

"Absolutely. Don't press yourself to succeed overnight. Honestly, I'm not surprised that you've found improvements to make in all three Woos. If you hadn't, I'd wonder whether you looked very deeply.

"Now, with a little progress every few days, in a couple of months you'll be able to look in your rearview mirror and see very noticeable improvement. And others will too," Frank added.

"That's very sound advice and I'll use it," I commented, thankful for a practical approach to personal change.

Hoping for some reassurance I asked, "Have you actually seen the Three Keys work for someone who has little or no enthusiasm anymore?"

"Hundreds over the years--literally. Some people I thought had little hope . . . James as an example."

"No, you're kidding," I said surprised.

"I'm not kidding. James made himself into one of our star performers, but, there was a time when he barely hung on to his job."

"James did tell me about some of the trouble his attitude brought him," I remembered. "He's a great example that anyone can build up enthusiasm and keep it. Talking to him helps me see that enthusiasm will make a huge difference in accomplishing my own goals."

"Fantastic," Frank exclaimed. "Listen before I forget, let me go get something for you," Frank said as he quickly left the office.

I took the opportunity to look over my notes about increasing enthusiasm and keeping it. These tips were just what I needed.

Summary/Getting and Keeping
Unlimited Enthusiasm

1. Overlook minor aggravations and disappointments--don't let them gain control over your attitude. Smart people know what to overlook and live on.

2. You'll have a better outlook if you'll stop to appreciate all your blessings in life. Make a list of everything you can be thankful for and reflect.

3. Build your enthusiasm by learning to focus on the positives in your job, your teammates, your boss and your family. The negatives will now be much less noticeable.

4. Never stop working on your enthusiasm. Make it a way of life.

Sharing The Woos

When Frank re-entered the room he tossed a miniature football to me and said enthusiastically, "Here you go John, take this with you as a reminder of the first Woo."

I almost dropped my pen catching the football. On it were the words: *Somebody--Nobody--Everybody.*

"Thank you, this is great--it will be a good reminder," I responded with a smile.

"You're welcome," Frank said as he took his seat.

"Hey," he said suddenly, "what about that promise you made me two days ago. Are you going to keep it?" Frank asked, smiling.

"You bet," I assured him. "I'll share the Woos with anyone who can benefit."

"Good, they're not meant to keep buried in your notebook," Frank said still smiling.

"Frank, I have the aspiration to write a book someday."

"Oh you do."

"Yes, I want to write a book that benefits front-line associates as well as managers."

"Front-line associates?" Frank repeated.

"Absolutely, I think too many books are written just for managers--and don't include the employees actually delivering the service to customers. They shouldn't be left out."

"Great observation John. I believe you're on to something. I'd be delighted if you wrote a book that helps employees at all levels. Everyone needs to know that they can increase their own success when great service is given to the customer," Frank encouraged.

I thanked Frank repeatedly for his kindness and willingness to share the Woos with me. Then we said goodbye.

"Keep in contact with me and let me know how you're doing," Frank called out as I walked away.

"I will."

On the way back to the hotel I began to picture how I'd permanently apply the Woos to improve my work habits and attitude. I couldn't wait to see how far Frank's secrets and my diligence would take me.

Many Years Later

The Woos worked great at my job--quicker promotions, more opportunities and rewards followed. Then several years later I opened my own business.

Now, I glance out the window and see customers coming in steady streams. The store is setting volume records again the third straight year. "Why do customers keep coming back? And why do they tell so many friends about us?" I asked.

"Is it because they get better prices? No. They pay a little more. Is the store more convenient? Not at all--many travel out of the way to do business here," I said to myself outloud.

I knew why so many customers returned. They returned because of the great service our people delivered. You could see the Woos at work in associates all over the store.

For one year I wrote consistently about the Woos. Hot off the press, I rushed the first copy to Frank. But, I really wanted to see Frank and thank him personally again.

So Bev and I went to St. Thomas.

Seeing Others Prosper From Wooing

"Muriel, you're as lovely as ever," I said handing her a yellow rose when I walked in.

"Look at you John, you haven't changed one bit since I saw you," Muriel replied blushing.

Frank suddenly came bounding around the corner saying, "John, how in the world are you? You look fantastic."

"So do you Frank," noticing that Frank had not changed at all. He still had that great tan, lean look and sported a bright colored islander shirt. Fantastic for being in his seventies.

Frank showed me down the familiar hall to his office. "John your book is fabulous," he said putting his fatherly arm around me.

"Thank you Frank, you made it all possible."

"But, you made the principles so clear--and it was fun reading too. I've already given a copy to every employee--they love it.

"Most read it through in the time it normally takes to see a short training video or two. Some are re-reading it, which I encourage of course. And it's helpful to have them read the principles I believe in-- but in your simple, entertaining style."

"That's great Frank," I said. "I'm very pleased it's helping your people--they're already top-notch on customer satisfaction anyway."

"Just because you know what's effective doesn't mean you don't need some good reinforcement. Besides, you know as well as I do, if you're not continuously improving you go backwards--and that's when your competition catches up," Frank replied.

"That's very true. By the way, changing the subject, how are Louise and James doing?" I wanted to know.

"Louise is a vice president now and James is our company trainer," Frank said proudly.

Then Frank reached over and buzzed on his intercom, "Johnny could you step in for a minute, I'd like you to see someone."

"Who's Johnny?" I asked curiously.

"You don't remember? You will as soon as...Johnny, here he is, come on in please."

I stood and turned to meet him.

"John, I'd like you to meet Johnny, our new Operations Manager. I believe you two first met on the beach when Johnny delivered newspapers on that route those many years ago."

I couldn't believe it--but it was him--same contagious smile and bubbly enthusiasm. "It's good to see you again Johnny," I said shaking hands.

"And you too sir," Johnny replied kindly.

After visiting with Johnny and Frank a little longer I said goodbye. And I thanked Frank one more time.

Then I rejoined Bev. She made me promise that we'd actually have a vacation this time.

On the way back to our hotel I couldn't help but think about how the Woos were still rewarding Frank's associates.

But then I couldn't help thinking about the affect the Woos had on my own associates. Anyone who *didn't stop* using them was more successful.

Others heard about our success and sought us out. And we willingly shared the Woos with anyone. We gave out copies of the book too, so they could share them with others in their company.

It felt very good to help. It felt very good to see others increase their own prosperity and become happier from Wooing Customers Back.

Just like Frank wanted.

The End

MANAGER'S PLAN TO PUT WOOING INTO PRACTICE

EIGHT STEPS:

1. Get everyone in your organization reading *WOOING.*

2. Talk about and teach the ideas and principles in your meetings "every week".

3. Clearly identify the service standards you want upheld.

4. Hold everyone accountable, especially yourself, to these standards.

5. Ask customers how you're doing--monitor service levels at least quarterly.

6. Quit basing judgments about service on primarily your observations. Reward and correct based on survey results and customer comments.

7. Be enthusiastic and positive about your people's progress. Celebrate any good signs you see.

8. Review *WOOING* using the principles as refreshers--do this at least once quarterly.

ACKNOWLEDGMENTS

My father taught me the foundation for great service: do the job right the first time and do more than your customer expects. His lessons taught me a basic but powerful life-long lesson.

Several others since, have influenced me. Clients, associates, friends--too many to credit individually. Their zeal for and examples of great customer service, gave me several ideas for this book. I am very thankful we crossed paths.

To my wife, who labored through the manuscript with me, encouraged, motivated, edited and most of all was just there for me as she always is. Thank you Jeanna.

ABOUT THE AUTHOR

MARK HOLMES, by the age of 22, had addressed executives at such distinguished corporations as Dow Chemical, Champion Spark Plug, Amway, SOHIO, Westinghouse, Southwestern Life Insurance and many others.

Now at 38, Mark is a frequent author and speaker-- training thousands of professionals each year from large multi- national corporations to fast growing small companies. He is often sought for consulting, training, and convention speeches on customer satisfaction, teamwork, communication, successful attitudes, enthusiasm and leadership.

Successful organizations like Tracker Marine, Commerce Banks, Bass Pro Shops, Silver Dollar City, Rhone-Poulenc and Dow Corning utilize Mark. Mark is the founder and President of two companies, J. Mark Marketing, Inc. and Mark Holmes Seminars.

WOOING CUSTOMERS BACK represents Mark's strong belief that improvement tools should be simple but insightful. And that real improvement occurs only with the support and conviction of frontliners and their managers working together. Mark is committed to producing interesting and valuable publications for this key audience.

Mark is devoted to his faith in God and to his family. He lives in Springfield, Missouri, with his wife, Jeanna, and their two children, Jaclyn and Jonathan.

PERSONAL NOTES FROM WOOING

5 MOST IMPORTANT POINTS I NEED TO ACT ON:

1. _____
   _____
   _____

2. _____
   _____
   _____

3. _____
   _____
   _____

4. _____
   _____
   _____

5. _____
   _____
   _____

READER COMMENTS

If you have a comment for the author of this book,
please send them to:

Advance Mark Publishing
P.O. Box 3175
Springfield, MO 65808

Or call: (417) 883-7434

Or fax: (417) 883-9492

Easy Order Form

☼ **Fax orders:** (417) 883-9492

☼ **Telephone orders:** Call Toll Free: 1(800)841-8540 (ORDERS ONLY please). Have your VISA or MasterCard ready.

☼ **Postal orders:** Advance Mark Publishing, P.O. Box 3175, Springfield, MO 65808, USA.   Tel: (417) 883-7434

Please send the following:

☐ **WOOING CUSTOMERS BACK**, $9.95 each. Discounts for 10 copies plus.

☐ **MANAGER'S COMPLETE DISCUSSION GUIDE TO WOOING.** You want to put WOOING to work now? This guidebook gives you proven session builders, easy-to-use exercises, supportive points and group questions guaranteed to help you get the wisdom of WOOING across to your team more effectively. You get hundreds of Mark Holmes' tested ideas and key points to energize your meetings with frontliners and implement WOOING quicker. Reproducible hand-outs, individual coaching tips, small group instructions--and it's easily adapted for meetings of 15 minutes to 1 hour. Hold over 50 great thirty minute meetings. 208 pages/looseleaf. $34.95

☐ **WHAT CUSTOMERS WISH YOU KNEW ABOUT SERVICE.** A complete seminar transcript of Mark Holmes' most popular seminar ever! Mark follows former President George Bush on stage at a marine World Dealer Convention. He presents dozens of ideas and tips to help boost your sales and bring the customer back--over and over. Mark reveals the eight most effective ways to exceed customer expectations--and explains three proven ways to terminate the most common killer to customer loyalty...plus much more. You get everything this audience learned in 90 minutes--at a fraction of the cost to be there personally. $14.95

☐ **YES,** I am interested in the possibilities of a Mark Holmes seminar at my company. Please send information about Mark's seminars.

Company Name: _____

Name: _____ Title _____

Address: _____

City: _____ State _____ Zip _____

Phone: (   ) _____

Sales tax: Please add 5.975% for products shipped to Missouri addresses.
Shipping: Include $2.50 for the first book and 75¢ for each additional book up to 10 books. Bulk orders shipped UPS.
Payment: ☐Cheque   ☐Credit card: ☐VISA ☐MasterCard

Card number: _____

Name on card: _____ Exp. date: _____/_____

Your Complete Satisfaction is Guaranteed!!

Easy Order Form

☼ **Fax orders:** (417) 883-9492

☼ **Telephone orders:** Call Toll Free: 1(800)841-8540 (ORDERS ONLY please). Have your VISA or MasterCard ready.

☼ **Postal orders:** Advance Mark Publishing, P.O. Box 3175, Springfield, MO 65808, USA. Tel: (417) 883-7434

Please send the following:

☐ **WOOING CUSTOMERS BACK**, $9.95 each. Discounts for 10 copies plus.

☐ **MANAGER'S COMPLETE DISCUSSION GUIDE TO WOOING.** You want to put WOOING to work now? This guidebook gives you proven session builders, easy-to-use exercises, supportive points and group questions guaranteed to help you get the wisdom of WOOING across to your team more effectively. You get hundreds of Mark Holmes' tested ideas and key points to energize your meetings with frontliners and implement WOOING quicker. Reproducible hand-outs, individual coaching tips, small group instructions--and it's easily adapted for meetings of 15 minutes to 1 hour. Hold over 50 great thirty minute meetings. 208 pages/looseleaf. $34.95

☐ **WHAT CUSTOMERS WISH YOU KNEW ABOUT SERVICE.** A complete seminar transcript of Mark Holmes' most popular seminar ever! Mark follows former President George Bush on stage at a marine World Dealer Convention. He presents dozens of ideas and tips to help boost your sales and bring the customer back--over and over. Mark reveals the eight most effective ways to exceed customer expectations--and explains three proven ways to terminate the most common killer to customer loyalty...plus much more. You get everything this audience learned in 90 minutes--at a fraction of the cost to be there personally. $14.95

☐ YES, I am interested in the possibilities of a Mark Holmes seminar at my company. Please send information about Mark's seminars.

Company Name: _____

Name: _____ Title _____

Address: _____

City: _____ State _____ Zip _____

Phone: (   ) _____

Sales tax: Please add 5.975% for products shipped to Missouri addresses.
Shipping: Include $2.50 for the first book and 75¢ for each additional book up to 10 books. Bulk orders shipped UPS.
Payment: ☐Cheque   ☐Credit card: ☐VISA ☐MasterCard
Card number: _____

Name on card: _____ Exp. date: ____ / ____

Your Complete Satisfaction is Guaranteed!!

Easy Order Form

☼ **Fax orders:** (417) 883-9492

☼ **Telephone orders:** Call Toll Free: 1(800)841-8540 (ORDERS ONLY please). Have your VISA or MasterCard ready.

☼ **Postal orders:** Advance Mark Publishing, P.O. Box 3175, Springfield, MO 65808, USA.   Tel: (417) 883-7434

Please send the following:

☐ **WOOING CUSTOMERS BACK,** $9.95 each. Discounts for 10 copies plus.

☐ **MANAGER'S COMPLETE DISCUSSION GUIDE TO WOOING.** You want to put WOOING to work now? This guidebook gives you proven session builders, easy-to-use exercises, supportive points and group questions guaranteed to help you get the wisdom of WOOING across to your team more effectively. You get hundreds of Mark Holmes' tested ideas and key points to energize your meetings with frontliners and implement WOOING quicker.   Reproducible hand-outs, individual coaching tips, small group instructions--and it's easily adapted for meetings of 15 minutes to 1 hour. Hold over 50 great thirty minute meetings. 208 pages/looseleaf. $34.95

☐ **WHAT CUSTOMERS WISH YOU KNEW ABOUT SERVICE.** A complete seminar transcript of Mark Holmes' most popular seminar ever! Mark follows former President George Bush on stage at a marine World Dealer Convention. He presents dozens of ideas and tips to help boost your sales and bring the customer back--over and over. Mark reveals the eight most effective ways to exceed customer expectations--and explains three proven ways to terminate the most common killer to customer loyalty...plus much more.   You get everything this audience learned in 90 minutes--at a fraction of the cost to be there personally. $14.95

☐ **YES,** I am interested in the possibilities of a Mark Holmes seminar at my company. Please send information about Mark's seminars.

Company Name: _____

Name: _____ Title _____

Address: _____

City: _____ State _____ Zip _____

Phone: __(____)_____

Sales tax: Please add 5.975% for products shipped to Missouri addresses.
Shipping: Include $2.50 for the first book and 75¢ for each additional book up to 10 books. Bulk orders shipped UPS.
Payment: ☐Cheque   ☐Credit card: ☐VISA ☐MasterCard

Card number: _____

Name on card: _____ Exp. date: _____/_____

Your Complete Satisfaction is Guaranteed!!